Family Life Illustrated

llustrated

WOMEN

RONNIE FLOYD

Family Life Illustrated

For WOMEN

RONNIE FLOYD

New Leaf Press

Family Life Illustrated for Women

First printing: November 2004

ISBN: 0-89221-583-6
Library of Congress Number: 2004106956

Cover concept by Left Coast Design, Portland, OR

All sidebar statistics have been provided by: The Barna Group Online, 1957 Eastman Ave Ste B, Ventura, CA 93003. (www.barna.org/FlexPage.aspx?Page=Topic&TopicID=21)

Printed in the United States of America

Please visit our website for other great titles:
www.newleafpress.net

For information regarding author interviews, please contact the publicity department at (870) 438-5288.

CONTENTS

Just For Women

A S I prepared to give the talk that eventually turned into this book, I asked myself repeatedly how I could speak and be heard by the girls, younger women, and older ladies whom I wanted to reach. That's my audience. How could I best connect with them to offer something of value on this issue that would significantly help each one of them in their day-to-day lives?

At first I thought I could say, "I am married," and thereby gain some credibility. The more I pondered the idea, however, the more I suspected that most women would respond with something like, "Your poor wife! I pity her; one would think she could have done better."

And I can hardly argue the point! I'm sure Jeana could have done much better (and all the people of God said, "Amen").

Eventually I decided that the only way I could ever be of help and ever hope to be heard on this topic is to faithfully take the Word of God, impart it as honestly and as skillfully as I knew how, and trust God with the results. And I have to believe that the girls, young women, and older ladies who have ears to hear *will* hear what the Spirit of God wants to say to them.

I tell you this right at the outset because much of what you will read in the pages to come stands in complete opposition to the cultural winds currently blowing strong and loud in America. I have looked to the Apostle Paul for guidance, for I know that he faced a similar problem in his own day.

An ancient predecessor of modern radical feminism flourished in the Roman Empire of the first century, a movement that the Apostle saw as a major threat to the early church. Two millennia ago, so many women were coming to faith in Jesus Christ out of a skewed background that the Apostle felt compelled to reorient their thinking according to the Word of God — which at many significant points stood diametrically opposed to the values and opinions of the prevailing culture.

So — if what follows offends you or feels like a threat to your present lifestyle or choices, then please take it up with God. I'm trying as best I can to be faithful to the Word of the Lord. Many voices out there call for your attention and allegiance, but if you consider yourself a *Christian* woman, you had better commit yourself to listening for and heeding the voice of God. After all, his voice is the only one that really matters — not Ronnie Floyd's, not the dominant culture's, and not even your own.

Once again, I hope that what follows encourages, inspires, and helps you. But if you find yourself struggling with some of the subsequent material, I urge you to talk to God about it. I mean that! Just go to Him and say, "Lord, how can I do *this*?" Deal with God about it. Bare your heart to God — because if He's saying what I believe He's saying, and if you deny what God says, then please know you are standing on very dangerous ground. I plead with you to be very careful and pray about how you will respond to what God may be saying to you.

Finally, I applaud you for wanting to take the time to ponder what it means to be a Christian woman in today's confused culture. And I pray that what I have to offer may give you some of the support you need to keep growing in your relationship with Christ.

Because that, after all, is the main thing.

Whatever women do they must do twice as well as men to be thought half as good. Luckily, this is not difficult.

– *Charlotte Whitton*

Chapter 1

Difficult Time[s]

for Christian

Women

THERE'S no getting around it: Christian women face a very difficult challenge in America today. Pushed in one direction by this group and pulled in another by that crowd, many women find it increasingly difficult to get a clear idea of who they really are.

On one side, radical feminism has encouraged women to see themselves in bitter competition with men, resulting in a never-ending war that makes every issue into a female-versus-male confrontation. This way of looking at the world often results in masculinized women who behave, react, and dress in ways more appropriate to men than to women.

At the opposite extreme, certain magazines,

For yet another group of women, the "hot look" is the natural option: sloppy, drab, disheveled. Put on anything you can find and don't bother to spend any time or energy trying to improve your appearance.

As a result of this boiling cauldron of competing ideas about what it means to be a woman, the lines between male and female have grown very blurred. Many want to make the two sexes the same in nearly every way that matters — functionally unisex. Revered biblical words like "submission" and "honor," therefore, have become hated targets, likely to stir up anger whenever someone dares to speak them out loud. Remember the furor back in 1998 when

television shows, and celebrities turn women into little more than objects for men to lust after and to fantasize about. So some women habitually dress in clothing that reveals more skin than it conceals. The immodest wardrobe of confused pop stars such as Britney Spears has become the *de rigeur* model for impressionable young girls.

the "family amendment" to the Baptist Faith and Message statement included the phrase, "A wife is to *submit* graciously to the servant leadership of her husband"?

All over the America, the views of Martha Stewart, Oprah, *All My Children*, Doctor Phil, *Good Housekeeping*, and even Jerry Springer have increasingly become the primary theological positions of the vast majority of women. And the Bible's perspective has become increasingly marginalized.

In fact, our culture tends to react in horror at the mere suggestion that a woman might find great fulfillment and personal significance by using her talents and energy to become — perish the thought! — a lowly homemaker. Honestly! We're told that such a thing amounts to nothing but an invitation to get walked on by her husband and mocked by her children.

That's the sad shape of the culture we find ourselves in — and that's one big reason why it's so difficult to become a confident,

> . . . our culture tends to react in horror at the mere suggestion that a woman might find great fulfillment . . . by using her talents . . . to become . . . a lowly homemaker.

self-respecting, God-honoring Christian woman in 21st century America.

Which leads me to ask two basic questions:

Question Number 1:
What is the role of a Christian woman, according to the Word of God?

Question Number 2:
Whatever happened to being a *Christian* woman? How should a woman who claims to follow Christ act and speak and think differently from a woman who makes no such claim?

I want to take a look at those two questions in the rest of this little book. But before I go any further, I figure I had better stop and make one important thing as clear as I can make it.

Women Mentoring Women

I have long admired the apostle Paul for a lot of things, not only for what he said and did, but also for what he *didn't* say or do.

A currently controversial passage in Titus 2 illustrates why I have such deep admiration for the godly wisdom of the Apostle. In verses 3–5 of that chapter, Paul instructs older women of faith to mentor and to teach younger Christian women. Why did he do this? Why didn't he insist that he, the great missionary and apostle, should serve as their primary teacher?

Do you know why he didn't? Because Paul knew that no one could understand the world of a woman as well as another woman!

Recently I came across an interesting list. See if you agree with its outlook on things. It's called "The Top Ten Things Only Women Understand":

10. Cats' facial expressions.

9. The need for the same style of shoe in different colors.

8. Why bean sprouts aren't just weeds.

7. Fat clothes.

6. Taking a car trip without trying to beat your last time.

5. The difference between beige, off-white, and eggshell.

4. Cutting your bangs to make them grow.

3. Romantic stuff like mushy cards and flowers.

2. The inaccuracy of every bathroom scale ever made.

And the number one thing only women understand:

1. Other women!

I may not know much, but at least I know this: women know other women better than I will ever know them. That's why I've asked my wife, Jeana, to give her own take on some of the most important issues we'll be tackling in this book. You'll see her personal, female-flavored perspective in the last chapter entitled "Q and A with Jeana Floyd."

I also want you to know that I've asked her to review what I've written to make sure that when I'm stating my own opinion, and not declaring what God explicitly says in His Word, that I clearly flag those passages. I don't want you to accept any of what follows merely on the basis of my own very limited authority; I want you to con-

sider it and make it your own only to the degree that it accurately reflects what

> *. . . do you consider yourself a grounded and stable believer in Jesus Christ?*

God tells us in the Scriptures He inspired.

And the very first thing I want to point out from the inspired text of Titus 2 is a very important principle: older Christian women are to mentor younger Christian women in the faith. Paul knew that women who had achieved some success in their spiritual lives would be most effective at training other women how to achieve their own spiritual success. So Paul describes what God wants mature Christian women to teach and model to their younger counterparts.

I wonder — do you consider yourself a grounded and stable believer in Jesus Christ? If so, then your responsibility as a mature Christian woman is to train younger women in the church to become what God wants them to be. All

The key thing is for . . . more experienced women . . . to spur spiritual growth and bring health both to Christian families and to the Church.

11 of the traits described in Titus 2:3–5 are to exist in the life of every mature Christian woman, but the last 7 traits, Paul says, are especially to be passed on from mature Christian women to younger Christian women.

Perhaps you say, "But I'm not qualified!" Listen — any woman who is further along in a certain area of life than another woman can mentor the less experienced woman in that area of life. You don't have to be a Bible scholar to qualify. In fact, the language the Apostle uses suggests that the "older women" are simply those no longer in their childbearing years. And the younger women who need spiritual mentors are those still in their childbearing years. The key thing is for older and more experienced women to come alongside younger and less mature women, in order to spur spiritual growth and bring health both to Christian families and to the Church.

I see so much wisdom in this simple principle that I think it's generally a terrible idea for a woman to seek personal counsel from a man. Time after time, I've seen unwise and hurtful entanglements develop after a woman bypassed older women for counsel and instead went searching for the guidance of a man. God says that older women in the faith are to make themselves available to younger women in the faith for most of the counsel and advice they

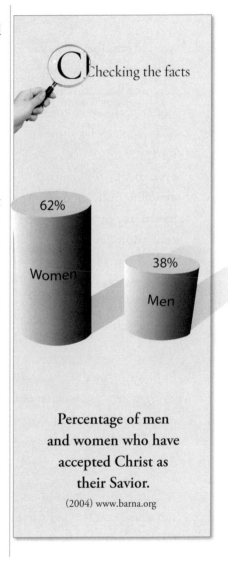

Checking the facts

62%
Women

38%
Men

Percentage of men and women who have accepted Christ as their Savior.

(2004) www.barna.org

need. A number of years ago, I decided that only on very rare occasions would I offer personal counsel to a woman who showed up at my office door (and even then, I follow strict guidelines: the office door has to stay open during the counseling session, etc.). If God says older women are to mentor younger women, who am I to say otherwise?

I don't operate in your world. To find solid and practical and intelligent help, you need to find a godly woman who operates in your world and let her mentor you.

Before we move on, I'd like to mention one last thing about this woman-to-woman mentoring. In general, it's more informal than formal. It happens in the ebb and flow of life more than it occurs in a structured setting. The people who have mentored me never sat me down in a counseling session and said, "Here's today's lesson, boy." The people who have mentored me have done so as I watched,

> *To find solid and practical and intelligent help, you need to find a godly woman who operates in your world and let her mentor you.*

The bottom line is, I can't help you beyond what God's Word says, because listened, and learned through their words and example.

That's exactly the kind of mentoring Paul has in mind in Titus 2.

This means that when you have a problem with one of your children, you go to your older mentor and ask for her advice. When you accompany your godly friend on a quick trip to the mall, you watch how she interacts with people and how she responds to problems. When you realize that you tend to say inappropriate things at unfortunate times, you talk to your mentor and see if she ever had to deal with a similar problem. In other words, tap into her gold mine of experience — you'll never know what bright nuggets are waiting there for you unless you carve out some special time prospecting the mother lode!

Trying to do the Lord's work in your own strength is the most confusing, exhausting, and tedious of all work. But when you are filled with the Holy Spirit, then the ministry of Jesus just flows out of you.
– *Corrie ten Boom*

Chapter 2

Four Things Every Mature Christian Woman Should Do

NOW we're ready to take a look at the 11 qualities that God says should take root and blossom in every woman who puts her faith in Jesus Christ. The first 4 are particularly directed to mature women of faith; we'll consider those in this chapter. In the following chapter we'll consider the last 7 traits that God wants to see in *every* Christian woman. Let's begin by considering what God's Word says in Titus 2:3.

> . . . the older women likewise, that they may be reverent in behavior, not slanderers, not given to much wine, teachers of good things.

If our churches had mature women of faith dedicated to living according to the direction of this simple verse, we'd see a revival that would shake the planet. Why? Let's take a look.

1. Every mature Christian woman needs to be spiritually healthy.

The phrase "reverent in behavior" means that you are to be honorable and spiritually dignified in both your state of mind and in your actions. In other words, you are to reflect holiness in all your choices. When people see you in action, they should see a reflection of the Lord Jesus Christ.

When God says you are to be spiritually mature, He is calling you to exhibit holiness in your choices, holiness in your attitude, and holiness in your conduct. The word Paul uses here calls you to live out your public life in the same manner in which you conduct yourself at church. There should be great consistency in the two. Your worship life

— how you behave and act on Sunday — should not look appreciably different from the life you live in the world. Your actions in both spheres must match; they must look like twins; they must walk side by side. God says that a spiritually healthy woman is a holy woman.

May I ask, are you a holy woman?

A holy woman loves to honor God even as she

Every woman who wants to follow Christ needs to know what it takes to become spiritually healthy.

loves to honor others. She conducts herself with grace and a gentle spirit, not with raucous inconsistency and harshness. She's spiritually healthy.

May I ask, are you spiritually healthy?

Paul called older Christian women to be spiritually healthy. They must strive to be holy, not by their own efforts, but by consciously and continually relying on the power of God through the Holy Spirit to form Christ in them. Every Christian woman needs to grasp the crucial importance of being healthy spiritually. If anything brings credibility to your life as a believer, it's that you are so spiritually healthy that you take great joy in helping other women to become what God wants them to be. Every woman who wants to follow Christ needs to know what it takes to become spiritually healthy.

2. *Every mature Christian woman needs to avoid devilish slander.*

What a forceful word Paul uses here in Titus 2:3! The Apostle employs the word "slander," which means to make a malicious, false, or defamatory remark about someone. In the original Greek, the word carries the connotation of "devilish." These words belong to the language of hell, not in the vocabulary of a mature Christian woman. God says that every mature Christian woman needs to avoid devilish slander.

When does this kind of destructive activity tend to occur? It always occurs when someone chooses to listen to gossip. It always occurs when someone chooses to listen to the slander of others. It always occurs when someone chooses to spread evil rumors. Scholar and author John MacArthur describes it this way: "This is a term used 34 times in the New Testament to describe Satan, the arch slanderer." Is it not interesting that the word used 34 times in the New Testament to refer to Satan is the same word used right here in Titus 2 about the kind of speech that, unless they're careful,

FOUR THINGS EVERY MATURE CHRISTIAN WOMAN SHOULD DO

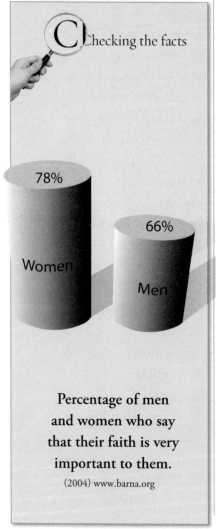

Checking the facts

78%
Women

66%
Men

Percentage of men and women who say that their faith is very important to them.

(2004) www.barna.org

can spew from the mouths of Christian women? That ought to grab our attention!

When a Christian woman participates in any kind of gossip free-for-all, whether by listening or speaking, God considers it a betrayal — that believer is allowing herself to be used by Satan. God calls it satanic activity to be a part of anything slanderous.

So be careful what you allow into your ears! Watch carefully what you say! Any statement that harms or could injure another — especially when it's spoken outside of that person's presence — is devilish slander. It is demonic activity. And

God calls mature, healthy Christian women to refuse to have any part in it.

> *When a Christian woman participates in any kind of gossip free-for-all . . . that believer is allowing herself to be used by Satan.*

3. Every mature Christian woman must avoid becoming a slave to alcohol.

The Bible says that mature Christian women are "not to be given to much wine." The passage here means literally to "be enslaved" to alcohol or wine. It means "to be confirmed drunkards." Spiritually healthy Christian women will not allow alcohol to take any kind of control over their lives.

This brings up a question for many people: Does the Bible teach total abstinence from alcohol? The simple answer is, no, it doesn't. But the Word of God does take pains to warn us about the dangers of alcohol, as in the following verse:

> Wine is a mocker and beer a brawler; whoever is led astray by them is not wise (Prov. 20:1).

The Bible strongly warns about anything other than God gaining power over a believer. Paul says, "I will not be mastered by anything" (1 Cor. 6:12). And the Scripture cautions Christians against marring or scarring their testimony for Jesus Christ through unwise behavior. "Be very careful, then, how you live — not as unwise but as wise, making the most of every opportunity, because the days are evil" (Eph. 5:15–16). Paul knew it would be hard for any Christian woman to be what God wanted her to be if she allowed herself to become enslaved to alcohol or drunkenness. At the very least, this is a matter of testimony.

I'm convinced that if Paul were here and writing today, he would have said something a great deal stronger than this. I believe he might have said it in this way: "Do not drink alcoholic beverages at all, because in your culture so filled with alcoholics and drunkenness, someone who chooses to drink cannot be a living testimony for Jesus Christ. You need to get yourself completely away from it and its influence, or sooner or later you will be associated with the evils of alcohol, which would dishonor Jesus Christ." Can I prove that? No. But I think it makes sense.

I'm also convinced that the principles of maintaining

> . . . a Christian woman who chooses to participate in any consumption of alcohol is jeopardizing her testimony for Jesus Christ . . .

a strong testimony and not harming the lives of younger believers through "permissible" behavior is far greater than any issue about whether to drink or not drink alcohol. Paul said, "So whether you eat or drink or whatever you do, do it all for the glory of God. Do not cause anyone to stumble, whether Jews, Greeks, or the church of God" (1 Cor. 10:31–32). I believe that a Christian woman who chooses to participate in any consumption of alcohol is jeopardizing her testimony for Jesus Christ to her children, to other Christians, and most of all, to the lost and the unchurched. Paul knew that in some hands alcohol has a strong tendency to bring dishonor to the name of Christ, and this is why he spoke against its abuse in this passage.

"But when we're in a business setting," someone says, "then surely we must participate with those who drink. It's just an expected thing in the business world."

Let me tell you something. I could name some very wealthy entrepreneurs who love Jesus and who have been active in our church for years — and they don't drink. They don't put up with it and they don't permit it. You really don't have to compromise on this issue.

Remember, the key issue is your testimony — and that is far more important than the issue of alcohol.

4. Every mature Christian woman needs to mentor others through her example and her words.

When verse 3 mentions being "teachers of good things," the word does not refer to formal instruction in the classroom, but to advice and encouragement given privately by word and example. It speaks of serving as a mentor, a trainer. The Word of God says that ladies need to mentor and train other ladies, through their example and their words, to do good things and to demonstrate good attitudes.

We must alter our lives in order to alter our hearts, for it is impossible to live one way and pray another.

– William Law

Mature Christian women are to train younger Christian women to develop God-honoring spiritual and mental attitudes. When a younger woman demonstrates a faulty spiritual mental attitude in the presence of a more mature Christian woman, God expects the older, godly woman to gently correct the erring, younger woman. This isn't just good advice; it's a divine command.

May I ask, are you willing to do that? Will you do what God asks you to do? Will you make up your mind to help train younger women in the way God wants them to go? Too many of us fear that we're going to offend someone if we should ever try to correct them. But regardless of the price, should we ever worry about that? If God tells us to do something, do we really have the right to tell Him that he should just butt out?

And remember that correction, rightly done, doesn't have to be harsh. It doesn't have to inflict great pain. When the one being corrected knows and feels convinced that you really do have her best interests at heart, even though the correction may sting, in the end she will thank you for it. As the Bible says, "Wounds from a friend can be trusted" (Prov. 27:6). Just make sure you're a friend and not merely a judge.

Chapter 3

Seven Things Every Christian Woman Needs to Know

ONCE the apostle Paul had addressed the spiritually mature women of the church, he turned his attention to the younger women who had more recently put their faith in Jesus Christ. And yet he did not entirely change his focus. After Paul instructed the older women to make sure they had built on a sound foundation of four godly traits, he then asked them to mentor young women in seven other crucial areas of Christian behavior. He directed them to:

. . . admonish the young women to love their husbands, to love their children, to be discreet, chaste, homemakers,

1. Every Christian woman needs to know how to love her husband.

In verse 4, Paul instructs older women to admonish the younger woman to love their husbands. To "admonish" means to advise, encourage, or reprove in a mild manner. Of course, to be able to successfully admonish others in this area, you have to first exemplify the quality yourself. In other words, if you're going to train another woman how to love her husband, you had better first take care of business in your own family.

If I were to ask you, "Do you love your husband?" what would you say?

good, obedient to their own husbands, that the word of God may not be blasphemed (Titus 2:4–5).

What seven things does every Christian woman need to know, according to this passage? Let's take a look.

"Oh yeah, I love him — he's a really good guy."

But you and I both know that, sometimes, that man acts like a jerk. Sometimes he's not easy to love. Sometimes he seems to go out of his way to create a stench in your nostrils.

Nevertheless, God's Word tells Christian women to love their husbands. Let's take a closer look at that for a moment.

> *God says that wives are to show affection to their husbands, not because they deserve it, but because it is His will.*

It is very important that we understand the particular word for "love" that

Paul chooses to use here. The original Greek word is *phileo*, which emphasizes affection. So Paul says that Christian wives are to show affection toward their husbands.

May I ask, do you show affection toward your husband? Or would you say that the "love" you show him feels a little colder and a little pricklier than that?

"But he doesn't deserve my affection!" someone says. "Listen, he is on a merit system with me, and he's not winning."

But where, may I ask, does the passage speak about a merit system? Instead, it talks about showing *phileo* love, affectionate love, with no conditions attached. God says that wives are to show affection to their husbands, not because they deserve it, but because it is His will. It has nothing to do with the man's conduct. God does not want you to tie your affection for your husband to some kind of behavior modification program — you know, to the degree that he changes in acceptable ways, you show him affection. "If you do this, then I will be affectionate to you." If you try that kind of approach, he'll never make it. I know, because I wouldn't, either.

This means that a cold wife — a woman who consciously withholds her affection and physical love from her husband — is out of God's will. This is not primarily a physical issue, or a mental issue, or even a conduct issue. It is a spiritual issue. Many younger women in our culture, even in the church, need mentoring in how to be lovers of their husbands.

There's not much wiggle room here. If you profess to have no interest in physical affection or sexual involvement with your husband, then may God help you and may God help your marriage! Sooner or later, your husband will look to get his affection from somewhere and someone else. You could hardly make a worse decision in your marriage than to neglect the affectionate part of your relationship. Such a choice will eventually jeopardize your marriage and its success.

It may sound obvious, but I'd also like to say that nagging does nothing to increase your affection for your spouse. And neither does it do anything for your marriage. Researchers at Peace College in Raleigh, North Carolina, recently discovered what they call the real secret for romantic intimacy: "Don't nag. Don't yell. If you really want to build intimacy in a romantic relationship, one of the most thoughtful things you can do is avoid yelling and nagging." Why? "In long-term relationships where intimacy is already established and has reached a stable level, positive responses to conflict do not increase intimacy any more. But negative behaviors, especially nagging, could easily lower it," they said.[1]

So learn to cultivate affection. Pile on the love, and don't forget the *phileo*.

2. Every Christian woman needs to know how to love her children.

The word *phileo* pops up once again in reference to a Christian woman loving her children. That means that mothers need to be affectionate with their children. God calls them to love on their kids.

Children need affection and unconditional

love from their mothers. This is God's will for every mother. According to the Bible, having children is one of the greatest of life's blessings (Ps. 127:3). Your children need to hold a very special place in your heart and a very special place on your schedule.

And it's not always easy!

That's why younger women need female mentors who will train them in how to love their children. I know very well that a lot of children are quite unlovable; sometimes even the sweetest children are very difficult to love. How do you keep on loving them when you really feel like strangling them? The wise counsel and advice of someone who has already gone through it can count for a lot. She can give you tips and guidance — or

> *One of the greatest things a woman can do for her home is to train her children to be self-controlled.*

maybe just a knowing, sympathetic ear — that can get you through the rough times. And what a joy it is to have her around when you can glowingly report more happy times!

3. Every woman needs to know how to be self-controlled.

The word translated "discreet" in verse 5 means to be sober minded, temperate, self-controlled. No wife and mother who lacks self-discipline will ever be able to rear disciplined and self-controlled children.

One of the greatest things a woman can do for her home is to train her children to be self-controlled. And the time to start is when they're young, because if it doesn't happen then, that woman is going to find herself listening to all kinds of disrespectful nonsense when they're 16, 17, and 18 years old. Don't put up with it!

"But I don't want to injure my child's self-esteem," someone objects. While I can certainly understand that, I'd also like to make you aware of an interesting study done a few years ago. Roy F. Baumeister, a Case Western Reserve University professor, spent years studying the choices people make. "If we would cross out self-esteem and put in self-control," he says, "kids would be better off and society in general would be much better off."

Baumeister and two colleagues wrote a book titled *Losing Control: How*

> *"Do what I say and not what I do" just won't cut it.*

and Why People Fail at Self-Regulation, in which they trumpeted the benefits of self-control. "If you can make yourself better in just one way, self-control will do you more good than just about anything else — it'll help you in work, in your relationships, and it'll help you stay out of trouble," Baumeister said.[2]

And of course, you can't teach your kids self-control unless you first develop it yourself. "Do what I say and not what I do" just won't cut it. A Christian woman needs to exhibit self-control in her conduct, in her words, in her lifestyle, her relationships, and her spending habits. Her life in totality needs to demonstrate self-control. That's the only way her kids will ever "get it."

A tall order? Certainly. But remember, you're not on your own to develop this necessary trait! Not by a long shot. Self-control is listed as a fruit of the Holy Spirit (Gal. 5:23). That means that as you stay close to the Lord and draw upon His power through the ministry of the Holy Spirit, God starts building self-control into your life. He also does this through the example of godly mentors, who demonstrate in real life what self-control looks like and how it develops. It's one trait that no Christian woman can do without.

4. Every Christian woman needs to know how to be pure.

Verse 5 uses the word "chaste," another term for "pure." A pure heart and a pure mind result in a pure life.

May I ask, is your mind pure? Is your heart pure? A Christian wife is to remain true to her husband in mind and in heart. That means, no fantasy for other men. No illicit dabbling in Internet chat rooms. You'll find nothing but danger there.

I must sadly tell you that some women in my own church have left their husbands after spending long and secretive hours in Internet chat rooms. Can you imagine leaving your spouse for some shadowy guy on the Internet? Well, it's happened — and it's not only happened with women, it's also happened with some men in my church.

Women have to be every bit as protective of their purity as men these days, because of all the godless home invasions that take place through television and Internet, videos, movies, other forms of entertainment, and the world in general. Men no longer hold a corner on sexual fantasies, for many women today seem as fantasy-driven as men. Too many explore their fantasies in ungodly books and videos and television shows, and give themselves away to premarital, extra marital, and even lesbian sex.

One of the greatest needs in the Church today is for women to make a commitment to purity.

A pure heart and a pure mind result in a pure life.

Be sure of this: What's in your heart will eventually become your life. So guard carefully both your mind and your heart!

5. Every woman needs to know how to be a good homemaker.

Verse 5 also tells Christian women to become chaste homemakers. When I got to this part of the verse in a recent sermon series, my audience suddenly got very, very quiet. This is *not* a popular teaching today.

I know that many consider this teaching about homemaking archaic. "It comes out of a dinosaur world," they protest, "and I'm far too sophisticated

> *The biblical idea of homemaker really comes down to this: God wants your heart to be in your home.*

and far too educated — far too 21st century — to lower myself into thinking that I'm to be a mere *homemaker*."

But maybe you have the wrong idea. What exactly does homemaking involve? Homemaking involves your work in your home — it's that simple. To further understand and interpret the term "homemaker," we have to take a trip back in time to the Jewish household of the first century.

In that household, the wife had to grind flour, bake, cook, nurse children, make the beds, spin the wool, launder, keep the house, and also take charge of hospitality and see to the entertainment and care of guests. That's a pretty huge job!

But I'm really not trying to make your home into a prison. "Keepers of the home" does not carry such a connotation at all. The idea is simply that you care for your home and guide its day-to-day affairs. So allow me to make a very important statement. Your number one responsibility — beyond your relationship with Jesus — is the ministry of your home to your husband and to your children.

I realize, of course, that as soon as I make such a statement, someone will say, "Sir, you obviously don't understand my situation." No, I don't. But in one very important way, I really don't have to. Because if God's Word says that Christian women are to be keepers of the home, who am I — and forgive me, but who are you — to say that God is wrong?

As much as I regret it, our culture has taught women to think of homemaking as despicable and self-debasing. The very word "homemaker" has become synonymous in this culture with terms like "oppressive" and "outdated." Listen — don't allow yourself to buy into such an ungodly mindset! It is evil and it is contrary to God's Word.

The biblical idea of homemaker really comes down to this: God wants your heart to be in your home. That's really the whole enchilada.

Still, the statement often leads to a common

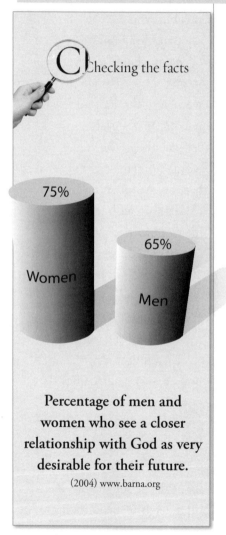

Checking the facts

75%

Women

65%

Men

Percentage of men and women who see a closer relationship with God as very desirable for their future.

(2004) www.barna.org

question or two. Should a woman work outside of the home? Should a woman have a career? The answer to these questions can be quite explosive, especially in our culture.

I would say that women who have a career or who work outside of the home need to understand one central fact: your husband, your children, and the care and guiding of your home affairs must take priority over your job and your career.

Is that really possible? I don't know; as I've said repeatedly, I'm not in the world of a woman. I'm not saying it is impossible; I hope it is possible. I trust that it is and I pray to God that it is. But only you can say for sure. If you can work outside of the home and keep your family affairs a higher priority than your job and career, then God bless you. So be it.

But if such a thing really proves impossible for you, and you continue to work outside the home anyway, then you have a big problem. Why? Because God expects you as a Christian woman to comply with this important part of Scripture. If you can't do that while holding down a job or a career at the same time, then . . . well, you have a problem. If working outside of the home keeps you from taking care of your home affairs, then your family will pay for it. I don't know how else to say it.

I do not believe that God says a woman cannot work outside the home. I do believe, however, that God says if a woman works outside the home, then she must continue to keep as her number one responsibility (beyond her relationship with Jesus), the day-to-day affairs of her home.

> *I do not believe that God says a woman cannot work outside the home.*

And let me say this, too. If a man is going to ask his wife to work outside of the home, then he needs to make sure she has whatever assistance she may need to help her to fulfill the priorities of her household. Maybe that means he'll need to hire someone to clean the house weekly, or otherwise help her complete her God-given assignments.

"But we can't afford that!" Maybe not; I already

> *When a wife willingly puts herself under her husband's leadership, she is doing something very spiritual.*

told you, I don't know all the answers. But please remember what we're talking about here: we're discussing what it means to be a *Christian* wife. God in

His Word sets that agenda, not me. I'm just reminding you of what He says. If you want to be some other kind of wife, feel free; but don't confuse it with being a *Christian* wife.

God bless you if you're working outside the home. God be with you if you're working outside the home — but if you count yourself a Christian, may God also give you the grace to understand that your number one priority, outside of your relationship to Jesus Christ, is the care and the guiding of your daily home affairs.

6. Every woman needs to know how to be an obedient wife.

Talk about jumping from the frying pan into the fire! If the last point stirred up controversy, imagine what this one does. But verse 5 really does say that wives should be "obedient to their own husbands." The word translated "obedient" means to be in submission or in subjection — in this case, a wife to her husband.

Warren Wiersbe, one of today's great Bible teachers, says, "While the wife is busy at home, it is the husband who is the leader of the home, so the wife must be obedient — but where there is love, according to Titus 2:4, there is little problem with obedience. And where the desire is to glorify God, there is no difficulty that cannot be worked out."

When a wife willingly puts herself under her husband's leadership, she is doing something very spiritual. She is covering herself with divine protection. And when she refuses to put herself under her husband's leadership, she opens up her life and the life of her family to the destructive powers of Satan. She makes her entire family susceptible to spiritual attack. That is one reason why it is God's will for every wife to voluntarily put herself under the authority of her husband.

Let me say it again: it is out of God's will for a

Christian wife to refuse to submit to the leadership of her husband, unless that man asks her to do something in opposition to the Word of God. It pains me to have to say that many men are nothing but perverts who would ask their wives to do some very wicked things — but don't you go along with them! Remember the rallying cry of the apostles after the day of Pentecost: "We must obey God rather than men!" (Acts 5:29).

"We must obey God rather than men!"
(Acts 5:29).

To willingly obey your husband also means that you will curb your tongue from speaking demeaning or disrespectful things about him, especially in front of others. A wife who lets her mouth run wild is in desperate need of some basic spiritual training. And who does God call upon to deliver such training? Again, He looks for a godly woman who will mentor that erring wife and who will correct her and call her to submit to her husband.

So, does submission mean that the husband is always right? Absolutely not. How could it? No mere human

is always right, and that certainly includes husbands. Without question, you have the right and the responsibility to appeal to your husband in a way that honors his God-given authority.

Many of us men need to remember that God often chooses to speak to us through the wisdom of our wives. Husbands have no divine calling to act like fools — too headstrong, stubborn, and rebellious to listen to the wise perspective of their life partners.

I think of the man who went to see his doctor. After some time, the doctor came in his room and said, "Well, I've got some good news and some bad news. The bad news is that you have an inoperable brain tumor. The good news is that our hospital has just been certified to do brain transplants. There has been an accident right out front where a young couple was killed, and you can have whichever brain you'd like. The man's brain costs $100,000 and the woman's brain costs $30,000."

The patient could not help but ask, "Why such a large difference between the male and the female brain?"

The doctor replied, "The female brain is used."

We men ought to be wise enough to draw on the remarkable brain power of our wives. After all, they are our fellow heirs and gifted creatures made in the very image of God.

7. *Every woman needs to know how to honor and live out the Word of God.*

The last phrase of verse 5 says, "that the word of God may not be blasphemed." That is perhaps the strongest statement in this entire passage. Older women need to train younger women to honor and live out the Word. Why? So that the Word of God will not be blasphemed.

When you claim to believe God's Word and yet do not live it out, you dishonor the Word of God and cause observers to sneer at the Christian faith. It is quite possible to slander God and His Word by the careless way you live; in fact, unwise believers do this every day.

Just a few verses earlier in Titus, Paul wrote of some professing Christians, "They claim to know God, but by their actions they deny him." And how did the Apostle characterize such pseudo-believers? "They are detestable, disobedient, and unfit for doing anything good" (Titus 1:16). Strong words!

And Paul has a similar thing in mind here. Christian women who hear the Word, but do not practice it or who take it lightly, "blaspheme" God and His Holy Word. It's as if they curse God to His face, live on camera and in front of billions of viewers.

Do you know why so many of the lost and

> *It is quite possible to slander God and His Word by the careless way you live.*

unchurched of America sneer at the Bible and scoff at Christianity? It's because they're watching us. When you say you believe but act like a garden-variety unbeliever, Romans 2:24 becomes chillingly true of you: "God's name is blasphemed among the Gentiles because of you." And the same is true of me.

Because so much is at stake here, I urge you to live out what you say you believe. Live out the Word of God as an older woman! Live out the Word of God as a younger woman! As a Christian woman, you should strive to model God's love so that each member of your family will honor and bless the Word of God, instead of dishonoring and blaspheming it. And when that happens, rather than a time for cursing, it will be a time of blessing:

> Her children
> arise and call her

blessed; her husband also, and he praises her: "Many women do noble things, but you surpass them all" (Prov. 31:28–29).

Endnotes

1 "The Real Secret For Romantic Intimacy," September 19, 2003, http://member.compuserve.com/new'html/live'scoop/cs/7.html

2 Ulysses Torassa, "Not to California: Drop Self-esteem," *The Oregonian*, Nov. 23, 1995, F7.

> *Christian women who hear the Word, but do not practice it or who take it lightly, "blaspheme" God and His Holy Word.*

The Christian faith is meant
to be lived moment by
moment. It isn't some broad,
general outline — it's a long
walk with a real Person.
Details count: passing
thoughts, small sacrifices,
a few encouraging words,
little acts of kindness, brief
victories over nagging sins.

— Joni Eareckson Tada

Chapter 4

Mary: Portrait of a Godly Christian Woma

EVEN when I have gathered all the relevant facts regarding some situation, I always get a better handle on things when I can see a picture. I love instruction manuals, but I like them even better when they give me an illustration or two. That helps me to form a mental picture of the goal.

With that in mind, allow me to introduce you to one of the greatest women ever to have lived on this earth: Mary, the mother of Jesus Christ. She epitomizes what a godly Christian woman is and does. She wonderfully illustrates what it means to be a Christian woman.

We get a number of glimpses into Mary's life in

the New Testament. We see her as a single adult woman; as an engaged woman faced with an unplanned pregnancy; as the mother of Jesus Christ; and as the mother of other children. We see her as a mother gripped by horror when she discovers how her son, Jesus, will die. And we see her at the foot of the cross, watching Him die.

Of course, Mary was hardly a perfect woman. No one should idolize her, or much less, worship her. But Mary is one of the greatest Christian women in history. And she lived in a way so contrary to our present American culture that she couldn't help but feel sickened by its sleaziness, saddened by its moral sickness, distraught over the deception it perpetrates upon women, repulsed by the widespread rejection of the teaching of her Son, and broken over the barriers that keep women from Jesus. She probably would find it very hard to understand how women could so badly misunderstand who Jesus is and what He gave His life for — freedom for all people, including the freedom of all women of all ages. In fact, no philosophy, religion, ideology, or any mindset ever cast has given women more liberty and freedom than the teachings of Jesus Christ and the Word He inspired.

And Mary kept herself pure during her engagement.

But back to Mary. What makes her so special? What sets Mary apart? What does Mary illustrate for us today? What can we learn from her? And how can studying her example help to bring about a spiritual revival of Christian womanliness in our society?

I want to encourage you, whether you're a girl, a young woman, or an older woman, that it's not too late for you, regardless of your age. Become what Mary was! And if you do, God will bless you in immeasurable ways. Note especially three godly characteristics that Mary demonstrated in abundance.

1. *A woman of purity*

Mary was a woman of purity. We see this trait in Luke 1:26–28.

> Now in the sixth month the angel Gabriel was sent

by God to a city of Galilee named Nazareth, to a virgin betrothed to a man whose name was Joseph, of the house of David. The virgin's name was Mary. And having come in, the angel said to her, "Rejoice, highly favored one; the Lord is with you. Blessed are you among women!"

The word "virgin" in this passage means that Mary had never had sexual relations with a man — and yet God told her through the angel Gabriel, "You will have a child."

Mary didn't dispute the angel's word (as the old priest Zechariah had a few months before, see Luke 1:8–20), but it did confuse her. How could it be possible? She had a fiancé, Joseph, but the two had never gone to bed together. As Joseph's betrothed, Mary was already legally bound to him as his wife — that's how it worked in the ancient Jewish world — even though sexual intercourse was not permitted in the betrothal period. Only a divorce could terminate her legal connection to Joseph, which naturally took the engagement period to a much deeper level. And Mary kept herself pure during her engagement.

The angel of God said to Mary, "Rejoice, you favored one, blessed are you among women." Why was Mary so blessed among women? She was blessed because of her purity and because of her innocence — the very things so many women have lost in today's culture. Purity and innocence often get ridiculed in our society. Label yourself a virgin on Leno or Letterman, and just see what happens. Women are under major peer pressure by our culture to be everything *other* than women of purity.

But it was Mary's purity that set her apart for God. It was purity in Mary's life that attracted God to her. Have you ever asked yourself, *I wonder why God chose her?* He chose her because purity attracts God. Always.

May I say something to you that this culture surely

will not say to you? The truth is, any man worth having feels strongly attracted to a pure woman who has not sacrificed either her mental or sexual purity. The culture may tell you otherwise, but don't you believe it. Purity is a powerfully attractive force.

So may I ask you, is your mind pure? Does what you watch on television help you remain pure, or does it cause your character to degrade and deteriorate?

Is your conduct pure? Are your ways pure before God? Do you dress in purity? With purity in mind, do you choose the kind of clothes that you wear? I hope you don't think I'm being too pushy, but shouldn't a Christian woman appear different in all ways, including her dress, than a woman of the world?

I'm not suggesting that you must put your hair up in a bun, wear no makeup, and wear a dress down to your ankles. I am married to a godly Christian woman and she doesn't look like anything from the past — and I'm committed to keeping it that way! A woman of great purity can still dress fashionably and look fantastic. But the most beautiful thing of all will always remain her purity.

2. A woman of favor.

Luke tells us in verse 29 and 30, "But when she saw

> *. . . purity attracts God. Always.*

him she was troubled at his saying and considered what manner of greeting this was. Then the angel said to her, 'Do not be afraid, Mary, for you have found favor with God.' "

Mary was a woman of favor — even though the angel's news made her feel terribly confused. The original Greek term suggests she felt *thoroughly* confused. Have you ever felt thoroughly confused with what God was doing in your life? If so, don't take it as a sign that you've lost connection with God or that he has some sort of beef against you. Mary was a woman of favor, and precisely *because* of that favor, she got some news that greatly confused her. In her deep confusion, the angel of God came to her and said, "Mary, don't fear what God is going to do in your life, for God has given you His favor."

What is the favor of God? It is the mysterious, sovereign blessing that seasons your life. It is amazing grace. It is something remarkably good bestowed upon you by a loving God. You can't work yourself up for divine favor, but you can position yourself to receive the favor of God. And how do you do that? We already saw how Mary did it. Her purity attracted God to her; purity always results in the favor of God.

And what does God's favor mean to you today? It means that, if you have it, you're special. You are favored. It means you are chosen by God.

Too many women today try to find

> . . . the only place a woman of God can ever seek esteem is from God.

personal esteem in their hobbies. They try to get their worth from the things they do for pleasure. Or they attempt to get it from the degrees they earn or the career they pursue. Other women try to get their sense of worth only from the nice things their husbands say to them.

Mary had it right. She knew that the only place a woman of God can ever seek esteem is from God. He is able to give you esteem like this world can never give it. Secure women in Christ get their value and worth and esteem from God and from God alone.

I wonder — how deep is your passion to have God's favor on your life? How much do you want it? The best thing you have in your life — the greatest thing you could ever receive — is the favor of God, the blessing, the special grace of God. And when you have that, you have all you need.

3. A woman of promise.

Mary was a woman of promise. Consider the words of the angel in verses 31–33: "And behold, you will conceive in your womb and bring forth a son." Don't forget, Mary was a virgin; she had never yet had sexual relations with a man. "And you shall call his name Jesus, and he will be great. He will be called the Son of the Highest and the Lord God will give him the throne of his father,

David. And he will reign over the house of Jacob forever and about his kingdom there will be no end."

In other words, "Mary, you are going to give birth to a divine, powerful being — the Son of the living God, named Jesus. The Lord is going to put Him in your womb, even though you have never had sexual intercourse with Joseph or with any other man."

That's simply awesome!

We learn from her response that Mary was a woman of the Word, and because she was a woman of the Word, she became a woman of promise. She willingly and eagerly walked in the word of God that the Lord gave to her.

Can you say the same thing of yourself? Are you willing to walk in the word that God gives *you*?

No one can say what God wants to make of you. The truth is, you could become a lot of things. Sad to say, many women grew up in unsafe homes that taught them not to trust men. Daddy abused them, or an uncle or some other male in their family or some other boy took advantage of them. Maybe that's your own story. If so, how are you going to deal with that tragedy for the rest of your life? Are you going to keep living out of that experience, with all the anger and bitterness in your heart that it created? I speak every week to audiences in which many ladies sit in the pew, all alone — their husbands have fled. So where do they go from here? Do they walk in bitterness for the rest of their lives because of what some ungodly man did to them? Does the world justify such a thing? Yes. Is it godly? No. The only way such a wounded woman can ever overcome any of her terrible pain is to become a woman of promise — that is, a woman who lives by the promises of God.

Are you living by the promises of God?

I know that my wife is. Five mornings a week, I awaken at 4 A.M., go to my study, and spend all morning with God. By 5:00 a.m.,

> *. . . Mary was a woman of the Word, and because she was a woman of the Word, she became a woman of promise.*

if I walk back through the house, I find Jeana up and reading her Bible, praying, listening to God speak to her. I'm married to a woman of promise.

The only way you'll ever be a woman of promise is to live by the Word of God and to let God put His Word in your heart. Spend regular time in God's Word. Look for God's promises. Make them personal. And pray that God will raise you up to be a woman of promise.

It's not only a promising life — it's the very best one available.

Chapter 5

A Choice and a Challenge

MARY illustrates for us what it means to be a Christian woman. The Bible portrays her as a woman of purity, a woman of favor, and a woman of promise. And it doesn't stop there.

In this final chapter I'd like to highlight two more qualities that Mary demonstrated in her life, admirable traits that every Christian woman should strive to emulate. And after we've finished our brief consideration of the life of Mary, I'd like to challenge you to become a woman like her. But first, let's consider two more traits of a Christian woman that Mary embodied.

4. A woman of miracles.

Mary was a woman of miracles — and what miracles she experienced! Consider Luke 1:34-38: "Then Mary said to the angel, 'How can this be, since I do not know a man?' "

One of the greatest doctrines of the Christian faith is the virgin birth of Jesus Christ. His sinless life hinges on His virgin birth. He did not come into this world from the seed of a man, but from the seed of our eternal God and King. That was the miracle. And that's why an astonished Mary asked, "How can this be?"

She got her answer in verse 35: "Then the angel answered and said to her, 'The Holy Spirit will come upon you and the power of the highest will overshadow you; therefore also that holy one who is to be born will be called the son of God.' "

It's an answer, all right, but it probably didn't satisfy all her questions. I doubt that it would for you, either. And so the angel put the capstone on his answer in verse 37: "For with God, nothing will be impossible."

Have you ever noticed how fond the Bible is of making this statement, or something very like it?

Way back in the time of Abraham, God asked a barren Sarah, "Is anything too hard for the LORD?" (Gen. 18:14).

In the time of Jeremiah the prophet, God declared, "I am the LORD, the God of all mankind. Is anything too hard for me?" (Jer. 32:27).

> *We serve the God of the impossible.*
> *That's why we can believe in miracles.*

On several occasions, the adult Jesus told His disciples amazing things like, "Nothing will be impossible for you" (Matt. 17:20) and "With God all things are possible" (Matt. 19:26) and "Everything is possible for him who believes" (Mark 9:23).

We serve the God of the impossible. That's why we can believe in miracles.

Let me ask you — wouldn't you like to become known as a woman of miracles? Don't you want to become a woman in whom God does miraculous works and whom God chooses to use in miraculous ways?

You may not know how God is going to do such a thing — but the "how" is not up to you. The "God of how" tells you in His Word that He is able to do it. He knows all about miracles and He alone performs all of those miracles. And the God of how says to you the very same thing He said to Mary: "The Holy Spirit is going to come upon you."

In your life, as in Mary's, the Holy Spirit is going to come upon you and He will overshadow you — not to make you into the mother of the Savior of the world, but to do whatever else He chooses. And therefore the very things that seem impossible for you to do, God is going to make possible.

I believe that my wife, Jeana, has been greatly used as a woman of miracles. The greatest miracle of all is that she has survived so many years with me! She has been a phenomenal pastor's wife. But greater than that, God has used her as a woman of miracles in rearing two boys who have a love for the Lord Jesus and a love for Jesus' church. What greater miracle could there be?

And it doesn't stop there. Jeana started a cancer support group, the Cancer Network of Northwest Arkanses, after she battled her own cancer back in 1990. For years she spent hundreds of hours with that difficult ministry. And now God has put a new burden in her heart: she's become a jail minister. She visits women in our local jail and ministers the Word of the living God to them. So if you want to hear my wife minister, get yourself thrown in jail in our neck of the woods. And then you'll hear a real woman of miracles.

Isn't that what you want to be? A woman of miracles? Choose today to be a woman who invites God's miraculous hand to operate in your life. Get busy now so that in the future you can look back on your life and say, "This is how God used me. This is what God has done through my life. Truly, He is a God of miracles!"

May God raise you up to be a woman of miracles. And may the God of how

come into your life to enable you to live by the promise of God, despite your questions. For if our Lord put the seed of God into the womb of a virgin so that she could give birth to the Son of God, then surely He is able to do all things according to His riches in glory in Jesus Christ, our Lord.

5. A woman of faith.

Last, Mary was a woman of faith. Verse 38 says, "Then Mary said, 'Behold the maidservant of the Lord. Let it be to me according to your word.' "

Mary willingly submitted to the will of the Lord, even though she had no idea where her choice would take her. Like Abraham long before her, she

> *Mary believed God. And God blessed her for it.*

stepped out in faith and chose to go wherever God wanted to take her.

That kind of faith is increasingly hard to find today. The late poet and author, Stevie Smith probably spoke for many when she said, "If I had been the virgin Mary, I would have said 'No.' "[1]

Of course, God never would have considered anyone with a faithless attitude like that of Ms. Smith.

Mary's submission to God shows what a wise choice God made when He picked her. She didn't understand how God was going to do what He said He was going to do, but notice her strong faith: "Let God do whatever He wants to do in me, according to His Word."

Is that your passion? Is that what makes your own

> *Mary's submission to God shows what a wise choice God made when He picked her.*

heart beat faster? Many of us continually seek advice from others, from television, and from books. But what about asking God? What about operating by faith and anchoring ourselves in His Word?

Mary believed God. The appearance of the angel turned her life upside-down, but she maintained a steady faith in God. Mary knew that if she would only submit to God's authority, the Lord would protect her. Mary knew the ways of God. Mary believed God. And God blessed her for it.

Mary knew she didn't have to prove who she was. She didn't feel compelled to carve out her own place in the sun. She didn't expect an unplanned pregnancy, but when God made clear His plan, she determined to cooperate fully with Him and receive His work in her life as a gift from heaven.

But still, she had some choices to make. What should she do now? Should she make her story known? But if she did, who would believe her? Since she already was engaged to Joseph, maybe she should move in with him and begin life as a married woman?

But Mary did not move in with Joseph to expedite matters. She did not jump ahead of the will of God. And so she confirmed her faith with a song of praise: "My soul magnifies the Lord and my spirit has rejoiced in God my savior, for

Checking the facts

70%

53%

Mothers

Fathers

70% of teens have daily conversations with their mothers about an important issue in their life, compared to the 53% of teens who have a similar type of conversation with their fathers.

(1998) www.barna.org

He who is mighty has done great things for me. Holy is his name."

I ask you today: Are you a woman of faith? Are you willing to go where God wants to take you, even though you still have a lot of unanswered questions? Do you want to follow in the godly footsteps of Mary, who provides a great illustration of what it means to be a Christian woman?

There's nothing keeping you from making such a choice. It's a big choice, I know. But it's also a choice that pays far more dividends than anyone can imagine. Remember Mary?

And now I'd like to challenge you to make that choice.

A Covenant With God

The Bible is peppered with covenants, that is, with binding agreements between God and His people. Normally when God made a covenant with His sons and daughters, He marked the occasion with a special memorial — a rainbow with Noah (Gen. 9:13), a blazing torch with Abraham (Gen. 15:17), tablets of stone with Moses (Exod. 24:12).

I wonder, would you commit to a covenant with God today? Would you agree to enter a binding agreement with Him to strive to be a woman like Mary and not a woman like this world? If you choose to enter the covenant that follows, you will, with the help of the Spirit of the living God, declare that:

. . . would you commit to a covenant with God today?

- You want to be a woman of purity.

- You want to be a woman of favor.

- You want to be a woman of promise.

- You want to be a woman of miracles.

- You want to be a woman of faith.

Would you consider going into this covenant with God? If your heart bears witness, I ask that you speak this covenant out loud, then sign it and date it on the lines below the covenant. Don't make this commitment unless your heart wants to! Remember, this covenant is between you and God — not between you and your husband, not between you and another woman, not between you and your daughter or mother, and not between you and me.

It's between you and God.

If you want to commit yourself to becoming a godly Christian woman like Mary, then speak the following words out loud and mean them in your heart, asking God to bear witness in your spirit:

COVENANT

As the Word of God is my authority, I choose to be a woman of God, not a woman of this culture. I submit my life entirely to the Word of God and to the will of God.

I choose to be a woman of purity. From this day forward will guard my mind from ungodly forces and choose the way of God rather than the ways of the world.

I choose to be a woman of favor. I receive my esteem from Jesus and His grace in my life, and not from anything else or anyone else in this world.

I choose to be a woman of promise. I commit to regularly read the Word of God. I will listen to the Word of God and walk by faith in the Word of God, ignoring the loud voices o my culture.

I choose to be a woman of miracles. I put my trust in the God of how, who relieves me from all my anxieties and who will do the impossible in me and through me.

I choose to be a woman of faith, for the rest of my life. I w not live by what I see or how I feel, but I will live by faith in Jesus alone.

Therefore, with everything that is within me, I magnify th Lord. I enter into this covenant with God, knowing He will great things for me. I rejoice that the Lord is with me. Amen.

_____   _____
Your signature   Today's date

If you just entered into this holy covenant with God, congratulations! You have joined a holy group of women whose intimate connection with God is giving them the power to turn the world upside-down.

And now, allow me to give you a parting word. One final characteristic set Mary apart from the other women of her age and from most of the women of our own age. Because Mary lived her life in the presence of God, she often paused to meditate on what God was doing in her life.

When Mary saw how the shepherds worshiped her newborn son, Luke tells us that she "treasured up all these things and pondered them in her heart" (Luke 2:19). And 12 years later, after the boy Jesus caused his parents no little distress by remaining behind in the big city of Jerusalem, Luke tells us again, "But his mother treasured all these things in her heart" (Luke 2:51).

Do you want to know what it means to be a mature Christian woman? Do you want to follow in the godly footsteps of Mary, the mother of Jesus? Then make it your habit to meditate on what God is teaching you. Treasure His work in your heart.

And then get ready for a grand adventure.

Endnotes

1 Jon Winokur, editor, *The Portable Curmudgeon Redux* (New York: Dutton, 1992), p. 312.

Q & A
with Jeana Floyd

Q: How would you describe the role of a Christian woman?

A: I believe the role of a Christian woman is to honor God in all areas of life, regardless of whether she is single or married or has children or doesn't. Her primary role is to honor the Lord in everything she does, whether

she's a homemaker or working outside the home. The bottom line is to honor God with all of her life.

Q: What kind of mentoring relationships have worked for you?

A: My most successful mentoring relationships were unplanned; they happened naturally. When

we try to force a mentoring situation, many times it ends up being very rigid and unsuccessful. The most important thing (and the beginning point) has to be a genuine relationship. Age doesn't necessarily matter, but you have to find someone who has a heart that attracts you. The way she lives, the things that are important to her, her value system — all these things have to appeal to you and make you curious about how she achieved such a heart.

Q: What have you learned or gained through a mentoring relationship?

A: One of the greatest lessons I learned from a mentor was the art of being a gracious woman. I saw the gracious way certain women honored their husbands in public, the way they carried themselves, the way they raised their children, the way they talked, the way they interacted with other ministers' wives — and those things felt very attractive to me.

Now that I'm a mentor, it feels so refreshing to be

with someone youthful, to be challenged and encouraged by their walk with the Lord and to realize how God can use women of all ages in a mentoring relationship. I often come away absolutely refreshed just by being with a younger woman. While I have the opportunity to pour into her life something that I have learned along the way, at the same time, she challenges me spiritually. And so I come away with a real fullness in my heart.

Q: How do you keep yourself spiritually healthy?

A: Obviously, you must spend time with the Lord on a regular, daily basis.

Then you allow other things to fall under that.

Maintaining a balance in your life, keeping all areas of your life under control — that's also crucial. When you live a life of order and balance, things just naturally seem to flow more easily. As part of that, I have to recognize all the facets of life that can pull me in a million different directions. Then I identify my priorities, judge what is important and what's not. That's probably one of the greatest lessons I learned years ago when I was diagnosed with cancer — after a situation like that, you realize that a lot of the things you think are important really are not!

After 14 years, it's still my check point when I feel like I am out of balance, out of focus, and things are spinning out of control. I come back to that and ask myself, *Six months from now, is this even going to matter?*

Q: How does spiritual health relate to emotional health?

A: The promise of eternity with God through a personal relationship with Jesus Christ — that is the foundation of everything. Everything stems from that.

It also results in inward peace with yourself — caring for yourself spiritually, emotionally,

> *. . . another result of being spiritually healthy is to be at peace with others.*

and physically, and maintaining balance in all those areas.

Yet another result of being spiritually healthy is to be at peace with others.

Another thing is confidence in the sovereignty of God, regardless of our circumstances.

These all tie together. When you know that you have the promise of eternity, that you have the promise of today and His faithfulness, and that you can rest in the sovereignty of God, those things working together will help you maintain an all-around balance.

Q: What's the worst mistake a woman can make in a mentoring situation?

A: The worst thing a mentor can do is to force her life or her particular circumstances on someone else. Everybody's situations are so different! Neither does it work to have a set of "pat" answers. It is much better to allow the

> *We should be as patient with others as we want them to be patient with us.*

person you are mentoring to search and dig for herself, to discover God's plan and path for her. I think one of the greatest dangers is that the person can become dependent on you and desire your life or your circumstances over her own, rather than totally depending on Him and relying on Him regardless of her circumstances.

Q: How do you respond when you hear a woman slandering someone?

A: I tend to ask, "Where did you get this information? And are you sure this is valid?" I try to help her see that difficult circumstances may have prompted the other person to react or respond in a certain way. I would encourage her to be more understanding, to refrain from passing judgment; none of us have the right to judge one another's motives. I would probably try to soften whatever the woman said and encourage her most definitely not to repeat it, but to check her sources and then to give that person the benefit of the doubt. We should be as patient with others as we want them to be patient with us.

Q: How can a woman show her husband affection when he doesn't seem to deserve it?

A: First of all, we don't show our husbands affection because they deserve it; we show them affec-tion because that is the way God has instructed us to honor them. If I'm in a teaching situation, I say, "You always honor your husband in public; you never dishonor him, whether he deserves it or not, whether he dishonors you or not. Of course, you have every right and privi-lege to go home and shut the door and have a frank conversation in which you express your feelings and your hurt, your frustra-tions, or whatever."

Q: What is the most im-portant kind of affection for children to receive?

A: I think physical affec-tion — hugging, holding, kissing — is so crucial. Another form of affection is affirmation. I think that is extremely important for children to receive.

Q: What is the best way to learn effective self-control?

A: Not to sound trite, but the best way to learn effective self-control is to walk with God every day and to walk in the power of the Holy Spirit. Unfortunately, that is easier said than done, but once you've walked down the road of life and you encounter the consequence of *not* using effective self-control, it's a great teacher for learning it! Knowing what the consequences might be for this or that action is a great way to learn self-control.

On the lighter side, one woman asked me, "Is it possible to have self-control around chocolate?" And to

that I must answer, "Absolutely not."

Q: What makes a pure woman different from others?

A: What makes a woman pure is what she chooses to put into her heart, whether it's the things she watches, the books or magazines she reads, or the things she plants in her mind. A pure woman will have a sense of conviction about when things are not right. A woman who is not pure doesn't even see it.

Q: How would you encourage a woman to embrace her job as a homemaker?

A: No one can fulfill my role as wife and mother

No one can fulfill my role as wife and mother any better than I can.

any better than I can. I feel a high calling to my role as homemaker; I believe I am the chosen one for my particular family. God has given me that great opportunity, and I can do it better than anybody else. When I consider my role a high calling and think of it as ordained of God, then it's easy for me to applaud and to be the cheerleader, because I love what God has called me to do. I feel honored that *this* is His plan for my life. I've never wanted to be a man; I have always loved being a woman. So I find total fulfillment in my job as homemaker.

Q: Do you find it difficult to obey your husband?

A: Actually, I don't. That might surprise some people, because my husband has a very strong personality. But I've always considered biblical obedience to be my protection. While I have questioned him many times, I don't think it has ever been hard for me to obey, because I so honor his position as the protector, the provider, and the umbrella authority in our lives. There is nothing in me that wants to get out from under that. I realize that my protection comes in submitting, and then the responsibility for the consequences, be it right or wrong, lie at his feet. It is a wonderful place to be. I do not have to bear that burden; in fact, I was not made to bear that burden. God made man first; He placed Adam over Eve, and woman was made for man, not man for woman. Once one accepts that and realizes it is God's plan, any kind of desire to disobey dissolves.

And what if someone says, "Well, my husband is

A woman who honors God will honor her husband.

not like yours. I can't have that same kind of respect for him and his leadership"? If you know what God's Word says, you realize what His plan is and you accept it and rest in it.

Q: Suggest a few simple ways to live out and to honor God's Word.

A: A woman who honors God will practice the spiritual disciplines, including prayer, Bible study, honoring the Sabbath, and sharing her faith.

A woman who honors God will live a life of purity.

A woman who honors God will be a good manager of all that God has entrusted to her.

A woman who honors God will know her priorities and live by them.

A woman who honors God will submit to authority in her life.

A woman who honors God displays a quiet and gentle spirit.

A woman who honors God will seek things of eternal value over the temporal.

A woman who honors God will honor her husband.

Q: What quality most attracts you to Mary, the mother of Jesus?

A: One of my favorite stories in the Bible tells about the relationship between Mary and Elizabeth. It is such a good example of the interaction between two pregnant women. In some ways, it's a mentoring situation, because Elizabeth was so much older than Mary. Mary was this young, pregnant girl, and yet Mary felt so excited to share her heart, her feelings, what was going on with her, with this older woman.

I think it gives a wonderful example of the relationship between two women going through very similar, yet very different, circumstances. One was young; the other older. One carried the Messiah; the other carried the forerunner of Jesus. I have always thought that God gave this story to us so we could see that even in biblical times, women loved to get together to talk about "women things." And it was a very "female" type of visit. I believe Mary probably spent a good length of time, perhaps several weeks, with Elizabeth. It wasn't just a day trip. That gave them time. I think women long for more time together, because they live such busy lives.

Q: How do you know when you have the favor of God on your life?

A: I don't think the favor of God means that everything in your life is perfect. We tend to think that if the favor of God is on someone, their life is bountiful and happy and full and wonderful. But I think the favor of God can be on you even in extreme illness. I sensed the favor of God when I was ill. I never felt as though God were punishing me. I never felt as if there were some reason I "deserved" my illness. In fact, it made me look more thoughtfully at things in my life. Finally I came to realize that, for whatever reason, God had allowed this illness in my life. And when I came to that conclusion, as crazy as this might sound, I felt as though God had chosen me to go through it, to bear it, and to testify to His goodness through it. I think I *did* have the favor of God

on my life, even when I was diagnosed with cancer.

I think the favor of God has been on us with our

> *We tend to think that if the favor of God is on someone, their life is bountiful and happy and full and wonderful.*

children. Not because we have been perfect parents! We say it had nothing to do with us. We have been very blessed that both of our children love God, neither went through a rebellious stage, and they both desire to be used by God. I consider that the favor of God on my life, and I've done nothing to earn it or to deserve it.

I don't fully understand the favor of God, but I know that I feel it at times.

I have felt it in my life and I can't explain it. I think it is easier for me to see it in someone else than to recognize it in my own life. I walk on that ground very carefully and very lightly. It's like talking about holy things.

Q: What promises of God mean the most to you, and why?

A: The promise of eternity is paramount. But as long as I'm here on earth and walking through life day by day, one of God's greatest promises to me is His faithfulness — knowing that whatever I go through, His faithfulness will be there to sustain me. That relieves a lot of fretfulness, stress, and anxiety. I know that He truly does promise never to leave me or forsake me, and that whatever it is that I'm going through — from the simplest to the largest matter — He is faithful. Many mornings I get up and whatever my stress point was from the day before, I look back and see His faithfulness to get me through that day. And then I have a whole new list for Him for the new day! His mercies are new every morning,

His mercies are new every morning, and I need them new every morning.

and I need them new every morning.

Q: What changes have you seen in the women to whom you minister in the jail?

A: I've not been in it for a lengthy period of time, so I can't say that I've seen miraculous changes. I have seen an openness to spiritual matters that I did not expect. It's amazing to me because most of these women have had very difficult lives. The majority of them have been physically, sexually, or emotionally abused. More than once I've walked out of the jail thinking, *Why wouldn't they be a mess? Why wouldn't they have totally destructive lives? Many of them have had to fight for everything.*

Just to see those girls grab their Bibles and bring their only blanket and sit on a concrete floor to have what we call "church" is pretty incredible. We give them a lesson and when we return the next week, most have studied it. Sometimes we end our time with singing. We stand and sing whatever they want to sing; sometimes it will be a hymn and sometimes it will be a chorus. But to hear those girls lift their voices in the jail cell is a wonderful experience. We have had a many as 12 or 15, ranging in age from 18 to some in their 50s. Recently we were ministering to a young woman who had to be there for 30 days — not long at all, in comparison with some others. She cried and cried and said, "I just don't know how I can do this for 30 days; I just don't know how." And I said to her, "You just take one day at a time."

Q: How can a woman increase her faith in God?

A: I don't think we work to increase our faith; I think it grows through day-to-day experiences and whatever we have to go through as believers. As we pass through circumstances and come out on the other side — as we witness the hand of God and see His faithfulness — our faith increases and grows.

I also believe that our faith can increase and grow through contact with other women — through mentoring, praying, and experiencing victories within a group of women. You're walking through life, facing all kinds of experiences, and you make a choice whether to worry or to trust the Lord. If you make the choice to trust the Lord, you see Him at work — and through that experience, your faith grows.

Lift up your eyes.
The heavenly Father
waits to bless you — in
inconceivable ways to
make your life what
you never dreamed
it could be.

– Anne Ortlund

PHOTO CREDITS

Also by Dr. Ronnie Floyd . . .

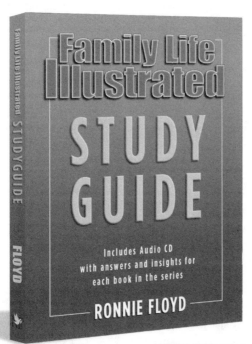

ISBN 0-89221-599-2

Special Features Include:
• Study questions in each book for reflection and to aid
  small-group study
• Study guide that works for all six books that also includes
  an audio CD from Dr. Floyd with answers and insights for
  each book.

5 1/4 x 8 3/8 • Paper • 128 pages
• *INCLUDES AUDIO CD*

Available at Christian bookstores nationwide.

Also by Dr. Ronnie Floyd . . .

ISBN 0-89221-588-7

Your job, your finances, your friends — nothing you ever do will matter as much as being a good parent to your child. Going beyond the surface strategies and quick psychobabble solutions, this book reveals solid, God-based insight on becoming a more effective parent. Don't choose to struggle alone — tap into the wealth of wisdom God wants to share with you and find how you can make a positive, remarkable, and lasting change in the lives of your children today!

Thought about your marriage lately? Or do you just take it for granted? Marriage is not a passive enterprise — it takes skill, work, and attention if you want it to survive in the "disposable" culture of our society today. Do you have the marriage God wants you to have? Tired of going through the motions, feeling helpless to make the change for the better you know you need to make? It's time to take control and make your marriage be the true partnership that God designed. Don't wait to make a renewed commitment for marital success!

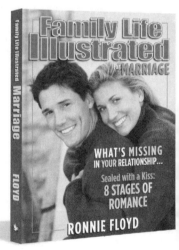

ISBN 0-89221-585-2

Available at Christian bookstores nationwide.

Also by Dr. Ronnie Floyd . . .

ISBN 0-89221-587-9

Money, debt, credit card complications
— believe it or not, the Bible can be the most
practical guide to financial management you
will ever find! Simple, easy-to-implement solutions don't require high cost solutions or pain-
ful personal concessions. Don't do without the
answers which can help change your financial
future and solve a critical area of stress affecting
you, your family, or even your marriage. Invest
in God's wisdom, and reap the blessings He
has in store for you!

The Gay Agenda is a compelling and compas-
sionate look at one of the most turbulent issues of
our society today – homosexuality and same-sex
marriage. Dr. Ronnie Floyd states the importance
of maintaining the traditional family, while reveal-
ing the homosexual agenda at work in our schools,
churches, and government. He also looks at the
ongoing controversies over gay clergy, and turns
the spotlight on judicial activism as well. Dr. Floyd
makes clear the political chaos and confusion of
this election-year hot potato as both major parties
seek to find political payoffs on these issues. *The
Gay Agenda* cannot be ignored.

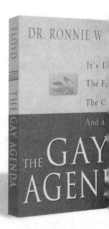

ISBN: 0-89221-582-

7 x 9 • Casebound • 140 pages

Available at Christian bookstores nationwide.